WOMEN'S AIR RAID DEFENSE

GRACIE
and the RADAR GIRLS

Written by Karen J. Moore
Illustrations by Lyn Meredith

Copyright © 2022 Karen J. Moore
Illustration copyright © Lyn Meredith

PHOTOS COURTESY OF THE COLLECTION OF GRACE HUDLOW ODELL

All rights reserved. No part of this book may be reproduced in any form by any electronic or mechanical means including photocopying, recording, or information storage and retrieval without permission in writing from the author and illustrator.

Library of Congress Control Number: 2022908428

ISBN:
Case bound   978-1-952467-10-3
Perfect bound 978-1-952467-11-0

Published September 2022

KC Monkeybug Books
Prather, CA

For more information, please visit the author's website
www.kcmonkeybug.com

Editing:
Linda M. Weller
Freelance Editor
experteditor@att.net

Art Notes: The illustrations for this book were rendered in red colored pencil, watercolor, and gouache. They were edited and enhanced digitally.

Dedication

In Memory of Janice Stevens
January 18, 1944 — June 19, 2022

"Be strong and courageous; do not be dismayed, for the Lord your God
is with you wherever you go."
—Joshua 1:9

For Gracie and all the women who served in the shadows.
KJM

******

To my grandparents, Marie Rough and Leon Coffman, who served in WWII and left a legacy of love and excellence for our family.

LM

That Sunday morning, I pushed through the front doors of our church ahead of my parents. I noticed a familiar group of young men standing by an open car door listening to the radio.

They looked at each other wide-eyed, as if something horrible had happened.

I marched over and asked, "What's going on?"

"Shh, Gracie. Listen."

A voice boomed, "I REPEAT, PEARL HARBOR IS UNDER ATTACK."

At sixteen, my world revolved around school, music, and boys. I'd never heard of Pearl Harbor, and I struggled to understand how over 2,400 people could lose their lives in a single day.

In the following days, the radio filled our home with more information. In President Roosevelt's famous speech, he termed the unprovoked attack, "a date which will live in infamy." He called for the declaration of war.

Our routines quickly shifted around supporting the war effort.

I couldn't imagine then the part I would play in an organization shrouded in secrecy.

    After graduation, I moved to Berkeley where I lived and worked at the Claremont Hotel. I heard whisperings of an effort by the military to recruit young women from the mainland to perform vital, top-secret jobs somewhere in the Hawaiian Islands. They needed intelligent, unmarried women between the ages of 18-34 willing to serve under a one-year contract.

    The lure of the Islands and the words, TOP SECRET, sparked my interest. Having no idea what the job entailed, I went to the Presidio in San Francisco and applied.

I underwent an extensive interview and FBI intelligence and loyalty tests. They informed me that I'd also undergo an FBI background check. My parents later told me that some neighbors had come to them and asked, "What in the world did Gracie get herself into? The FBI's asking questions about her."

The Army accepted me despite whatever naughty infractions I imagined they had found. After a complete physical, my orders were to go by train from Berkeley to Seattle, Washington and wait for further instructions. I was to tell no one.

Word came a few days later. Countless soldiers, nurses, Red Cross volunteers, and six new recruits, including myself, gathered at the dock in the cold, early morning hours. I buttoned up my courage and ascended the gangway to board a crowded Liberty ship.

One large room, reserved for the females on board, burst with Army-style cots stacked three high. As the youngest, I was crammed in the middle. The vessel zig-zagged across the rough Pacific Ocean to avoid any possible detection by enemies lurking below or above the waterline.

The first arrow of fear struck as we approached the camouflaged and blacked-out lighthouse at the Honolulu Harbor, the Aloha Tower. My heart pounded when I observed burned-out structures and bullet-riddled buildings. The realities of a war zone settled deep into my bones. The palm trees swaying to the fragrant ocean breeze stood in strong contrast to the destruction, as did my emotions. The swirl of fear and excitement left me uneasy.

An Army Lieutenant escorted us to the Iolani Palace, the center of government for the Territory of Hawaii. They briefed us on the censorship of all mail, incoming and outgoing; our living quarters at Fort Shafter; work stations; training; food buying; salary; required uniforms … both fatigue and dress; and the strictly enforced 10:00pm curfew. We were now members of the Women's Air Raid Defense (WARD), part of the 7th Fighter Wing, under the command of Brigadier General John Weikert.

After arriving at Ft. Shafter, we toured our assigned quarters, which had formerly been used for officers' families.

A supervisor led us behind our quarters, up a hill, and across a small bridge where an armed guard met us in front of a large metal door. It opened to a huge swell in the earth where our workplace waited. We were deep underground in a secret, bomb-proof tunnel, code named "LIZARD."

My jaw dropped at the enormity of it. The tunnel contained many rooms, but the hub of activity was in the main plotting room. There we'd be assigned shifts after completing intense training in a replicated room.

First, we had to master a highly complex warning system based on the technology of radar: Radio Air Detection And Ranging.

The instructor stressed, "You'll be receiving details of all air traffic over the islands in the Hawaiian chain, 24 hours-a-day, every day, using RADAR."

    Girls stood on all four sides of a huge plotting table which displayed a map of the Hawaiian Islands. Large coded grids sectioned into smaller grids were superimposed onto the map.

    Through headsets, we received data to give the location, speed, and number of aircraft and surface craft. A plot was given through each radar antenna station located around the island of Oahu by a person code named, "Oscar." We replied with our code name, "Oscar, this is Rascal. I read you loud and clear." As other plots came in at regular intervals, it established the speed of the approach.

As data came in, we used colored markers to give them identifying numbers, dates, number of vessels or planes, and type. We used a plotting rake with a rubber tip, similar to a shuffleboard stick, to move our markers.

They called us Shuffleboard Pilots.

With training complete and nerves under control, we moved to the plotting room with a new sense of urgency and confidence in our ability to perform well under extreme pressure.

Identification, friend or foe (IFF) was used to identify bogeys, or enemy aircraft. Failure to identify caused quick action in the plotting room, with blackout conditions and infantrymen in full battle dress lining the street up to the entrance of the tunnel. Key members of all the agencies came to the plotting room to monitor the activity.

We worked six-hour shifts, rotating counter-clockwise every two days, with a thirty-six-hour break after six days. I don't remember anyone ever being late for their shift.

Beyond the plotting room was a snack bar where, during our fifteen-minute breaks, we ordered spam sandwiches and Cokes, or donuts and coffee. Due to rationing and our location, fresh food was hard to get. But it was a cozy spot to relax, laugh with our co-workers, and clear our heads of the stressful, no-nonsense plotting room where lives depended on our accuracy.

Past the snack bar, an escape door waited to be opened in the event of an emergency or invasion. We were assigned officer status to ensure better and safer treatment in case of capture. After mastering our craft and proving our worth as plotters, we were awarded our set of gold wings, pinned over the left breast pocket of our pale blue uniform. I wore mine with great pride.

We enjoyed an active social life while not on duty. I recall the first formal party I attended at the Officer's Club for the Central Command. Early in the evening, a bug had entered the upper front of my dress and began crawling around. You can imagine my embarrassment as I tried to discreetly cast off the pesky intruder. When an officer noticed my obvious dilemma, he swiftly escorted me to another building where I removed the invader in private. From that time forward my nickname was "Bugs."

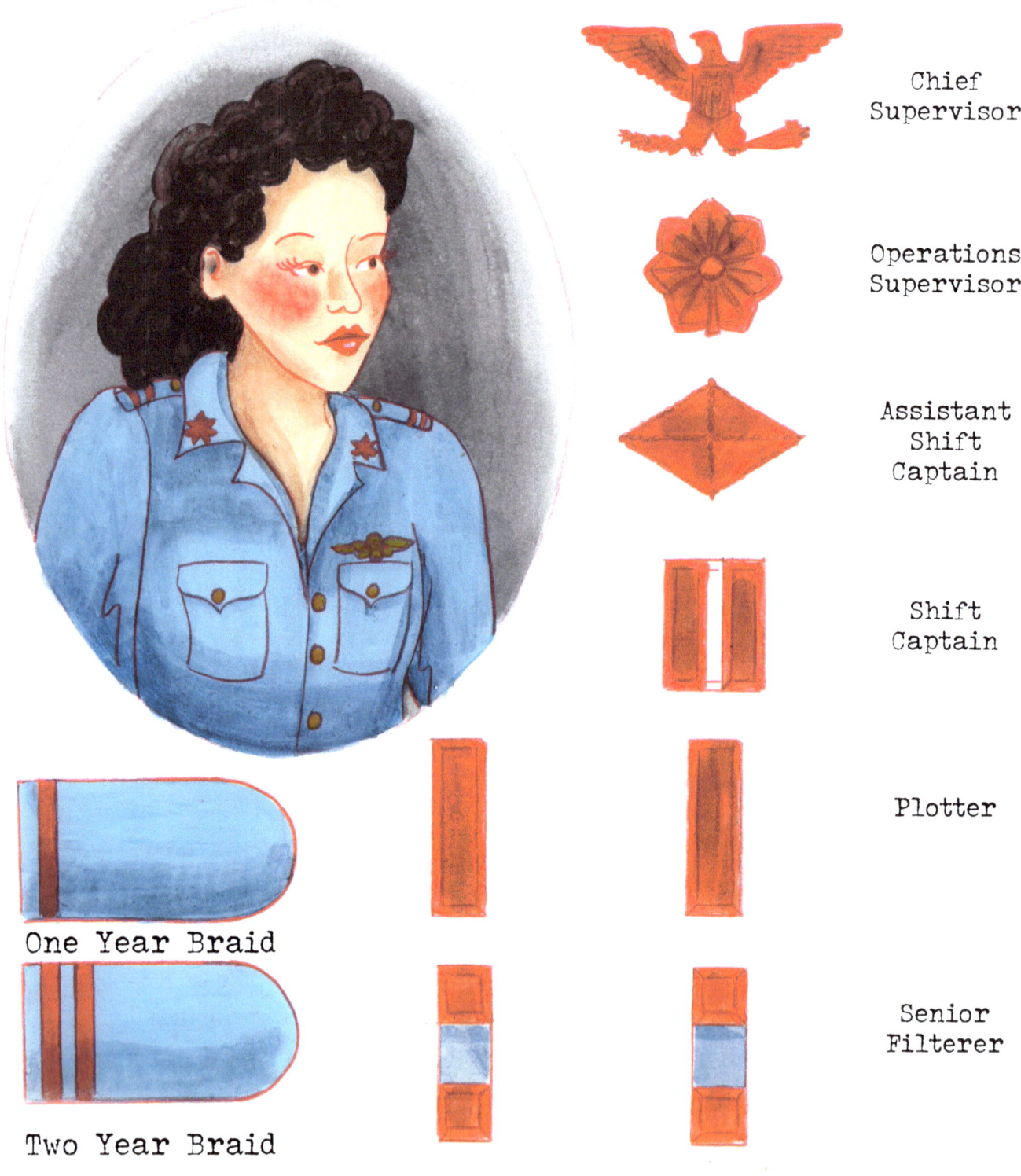

The WARD entailed a number of responsibilities, specialized jobs, and ranks, such as Senior Plotter, Filterer, Senior Filterer, Assistant Shift Captain, Operations Supervisor, and Chief Supervisor. Each job required a new skill set, intense training, and a greater understanding of math, science, and the technology of radar.

Shifts in the tunnel also consisted of air-sea rescue operations and interceptor pilot training. Pilot drills took place night and day until trainees were ready to be sent to the forward bases. We took satisfaction in knowing that the professional and precise execution of our jobs saved lives, while protecting the islands and ultimately, the mainland.

Respect for the women who served before me grew when I imagined them during the nightly air-raids in the weeks and months following the attack on Pearl Harbor and standing their post during the battle of Midway.

On September 2, 1945, while on duty, I was told to exit the tunnel through the escape doors at an exact time. We went out onto the swinging rope bridge high above the blacked-out city of Honolulu. At the announced time, the night came alive when the street lights all over the island turned on and searchlights arced across the sky in celebration. Tears of joy streamed down my face as I witnessed the most glorious sight I'd ever seen.

The War Was Over!

On October 14, 1945, I was among 200 servicewomen boarding the SS Monterey bound for home.

A Marine Corps band serenaded us, first with Anchors Aweigh, then with The Marine Corps Hymn, and finally with the Coast Guard Song.

An honor guard of 36 Navy men, 36 Coast Guardsmen, and 36 Marines stood at attention as we filed onto the ship.

The SS Monterey docked in San Francisco the following Friday, where we were greeted with a civic welcome home.

My senior year at
Modesto High 42-43

Is Betrothed To Lieutenant

And another engagement!

Friends here of Miss Grace Hudlow are learning of her engagement to Lieutenant Oliver L. Kincanon of Bellview, Texas.

Daughter of Mr. and Mrs. H. H. Hudlow of this city, the bride elect is a senior student at Modesto High School.

Lieutenant Kincannon, the son of Mr. and Mrs. J. L. Kincanon of Bluffdale, Texas, attended the University of Texas and was commissioned early last month from Stockton Field. He was a member of the Royal Canadian Air Force for nine months, and is now at Rogers Field, Oklahoma

I lost my dear Oliver to war on March 12, 1943.

On the way to Honolulu

US Army Forces in the Central Pacific Area Women's Air Raid Defense

WARD around the plotting table at LIZARD

Enjoying R&R

Dinner with these handsome fellas

WARD banquet at Hickam Field. Colonel Kitty Coonley, Lt. Gen. Richardson, Capt. Weegie Abbott and Brig. Gen. Wiekert (7th Fighter Wing)

Our view from the bridge of the glorius light display.

NOLULU ADVERTISER, MONDAY MORNING, OCTOBER 15, 1945.

REE MEMBERS of the now-disbanded Women's Air Raid Defense wave goodbye to friend Left to right, Barbara Germaine, 24, Oakland, Calif.; Virginia Lane, 24, San Franc llow, 21, Modesto, Calif.

Virginia Lane and me on board the S.S. Monterey

Going home. Oct. 14, 1945

HEADQUARTERS 7TH FIGHTER WING AAF
OFFICE OF THE COMMANDING GENERAL
APO 958

In reply refer to:

18 October 1945

Miss Grace Hudlow
228 Yosemite Ave.
Modesto, California

Dear Miss Hudlow:

It is hoped that the enclosed pictures of the Aloha Party given for Mrs. Coonley when she retired from the Women's Air Raid Defense organization and the pictures of your departure from the Island of Oahu will be of interest to you and will bring back many pleasant memories of your stay here in the Islands.

Your work in connection with the operation of the Air Defense System of the Hawaiian Islands was outstanding. I wish to take this opportunity again to express my personal appreciation for your untiring efforts while employed here.

I trust that your voyage home was a most pleasant one and that your future holds nothing but the best of everything.

Sincerely yours,

JOHN M. WEIKERT,
Brigadier General, U. S. Army,
Commanding.

Encls.

WARD reunion 1981. The radar girls came from all different backgrounds, representing the islands and most states. We bonded under a common goal and made life-long friendships.

THE HISTORY OF
THE WOMEN'S AIR RAID DEFENSE
AT FORT SHAFTER

December 7, 1941
Honolulu, HI
The Japanese bomb Pearl Harbor in an unprovoked attack.

December 26, 1941
Royal Hawaiian Hotel
With the men called to forward battle, General Davidson holds a covert meeting with a select group of women chosen for their intelligence and loyalty. They're recruited to participate in a top-secret project.

January 1, 1942
Iolani Palace
The Women's Air Raid Defense (WARD) forms, and their training in the field of radar begins. Many of the men are shocked by the prospect and unprecedented replacement of active military men with civilian women.

January 12, 1942
Fort Shafter
The WARD proceeds to work their first night shift inside a temporary building code-named LITTLE ROBERT.

February 1, 1942
The WARD takes over duty in the plotting room around the clock.

May 12, 1942
The WARDs move into their permanent work location in an underground tunnel code-named LIZARD.

June 1942
Battle of Midway
Following the battle of Midway, the Army establishes air defense operation centers on surrounding islands. The WARD staff the additional centers.

June 13, 1943
Fort Shafter
The WARD detaches from the Signal Corps to become the WARD UNIT of the 7th Fighter Command and later the 7th Fighter Wing.

1943
San Francisco
A recruitment effort for new WARD members begins on the mainland. The Army still classifies air defense top-secret, so the recruits experience cloak-and-dagger meetings, loyalty tests, intelligence tests, and FBI back-ground checks, before being accepted.

February 1943
Honolulu, HI
Thirty-four mainland recruits arrive by ship with an additional 4 to 8 recruits due to arrive each month. WARD experiences adequate strength in numbers for the first time.

October, 1944
Seattle, WA
Gracie and 5 other recruits board a Liberty Ship to join the WARD at Fort Shafter.

September 2, 1945
The surrender of Imperial Japan is officially signed, bringing World War II to an end.

September 27, 1945
LIZARD
The remaining WARD members stand their last shift.

October 14, 1945
Honolulu, HI
Gracie is among 200 servicewomen, including 87 members of the WARD, who board the SS Monterey bound for San Francisco.

RESOURCES

Oral interviews and personal writings of Grace Hudlow Odell

SHUFFLEBOARD PILOTS: THE HISTORY OF THE WOMEN'S AIR RAID DEFENSE IN HAWAII, 1941-1945 by: Candace A. Chenoweth and A. Kam Napier

Honolulu Star Bulletin, Friday, February 6, 1942

The Honolulu Advertiser, Sunday, November 1, 1942

The Honolulu Advertiser, Wednesday, November 4, 1942

Honolulu Star Bulletin, Tuesday, December, 1942

The Honolulu Advertiser, Sunday, February 14, 1943

Honolulu Star Bulletin, Tuesday, September 7, 1943

The Honolulu Advertiser, Thursday, January 27, 1944

The Honolulu Advertiser, Wednesday, March 28, 1945

The Honolulu Advertiser, Sunday, September 30, 1945

The Honolulu Advertiser, Sunday, October 14, 1945

The Honolulu Advertiser, Monday morning, October 15, 1945

Honolulu Star Bulletin, Saturday, October 20, 1945

The Modesto Bee, Sunday, November 19, 1972

Honolulu Star Bulletin, Thursday, December 11, 2003

en.wikipedia.org/wiki/Women's_Air_Raid_Defense

The Women's Air Raid Defense: Protecting the Hawaiian Islands/Aviation History Magazine/May 2002/Ronald R. Gilliam

U.S. Women's Air Raid Defense Military History Forum, Discussion in "Regiment Histories" stated by: Kyt, November 12, 2007, Intrepid Cambria Woman manned radar in World War II

"Attack At Pearl Harbor, 1941," EyeWitness – history through the eyes of those who lived it, www.ibiscom.com (1997).

The McHenry Museum, Modesto, CA. volunteer: Janet Lancaster

Fresno County Library Heritage Room - Melissa Scroggins

Lyn Meredith is the illustrator of several children's books. She has won book awards for *The Water Princess* and *Home*. As well as illustrating children's books, she also does illustration and animation for a tech company. She lives with her husband, her horses, cows, and cats on a ranch in Central California. To learn more about her work, please visit www.lynmeredith.com.

Karen interviewing Gracie at her home in Fresno, CA.
RIP Grace Inger Hudlow Odell 3/13/1925 — 05/15/2020

This is Karen's sixth published picture book, her other titles include: *PEN THE TALE, OOGIE – A STORY FOR CLEOCATRA* – and the award-winning *CAR SHOW COUNTDOWN.*

To see more about Karen and her books, please visit: www.kcmonkeybug.com

www.ingramcontent.com/pod-product-compliance
Lightning Source LLC
Chambersburg PA
CBHW050751110526
44592CB00002B/32